green leaf

brown bear

purple pencils

orange carrot

How you can help

First Steps *colours and shapes* helps children to recognise and name the main colours and shapes. Appealing photographs enable them to relate the colours and shapes to things they see around them every day.

 Enjoy talking about the photographs together. Does your child have a mug? Is it red, like the one in the book?

 When she* shows an interest, focus on the colours and shapes. Help her to spot similarities and differences.

There are lots of other ways you can help your child to learn about colours and shapes. Discussing favourite colours whilst painting, dressing, etc will help to boost your child's interest, learning and confidence.

Ask your child what shapes she can see in the house, in the street or at the shops. Encourage her to talk about what shapes she can see around her.

*To avoid the clumsy 'he/she',
the child is referred to throughout as 'she'.

Ladybird would like to thank Priscilla Hannaford, freelance editor on this series.

A catalogue record for this book is available
from the British Library

Published by Ladybird Books Ltd
A subsidiary of the Penguin Group
A Pearson Company
© LADYBIRD BOOKS LTD MCMXCVII

LADYBIRD and the device of a Ladybird are trademarks of
Ladybird Books Ltd Loughborough Leicestershire UK

*All rights reserved. No part of this publication may be reproduced,
stored in a retrieval system, or transmitted in any form or by any means,
electronic, mechanical, photocopying, recording or otherwise,
without the prior consent of the copyright owner.*

colours and
shapes

by Lesley Clark
photography by Garie Hind
illustrations by Terry Burton

Everything has a colour. There are colours of things to play with...

colours of things to eat...

colours of things in your home...

and colours of things
in the street.

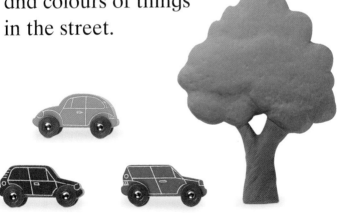

How many different colours
can you see?

Boots, coat, ribbons, hat –
I'm dressed all in red!

Let's hunt for some more red!

red apple

red bus

red mug   red play dough

Yellow is bright, bold and fun. Yellow
is the colour of my sun.

Here are lots of yellow things.

yellow banana

yellow jumper

yellow duck

yellow sponge

Blue dress for a blue-sky day. Why don't you come out and play?

Discuss with your child the different shades of blue she can see. Explain to her that we call all these colours 'blue'.

Point to the blue things you
can play with.

blue cap

blue bricks

blue paper
and crayons

blue car

Green is bright, just like a tree.
I think green looks great on me.

When you are in the garden or the park, look for different shades of green. Use words like 'lighter', 'paler', 'darker', etc to describe them.

What green things can you see here?

green T-shirt

green painting

green
watering can

green leaf

Can you tidy your own toys into groups and colours?

blue

red

Look at all the colours on the train!

yellow

green

What colour is the funnel?

What colour is the roof?

Mixing paints is so much fun.

red

blue

purple

Red and blue make purple.

red

yellow

orange

Red and yellow make orange.

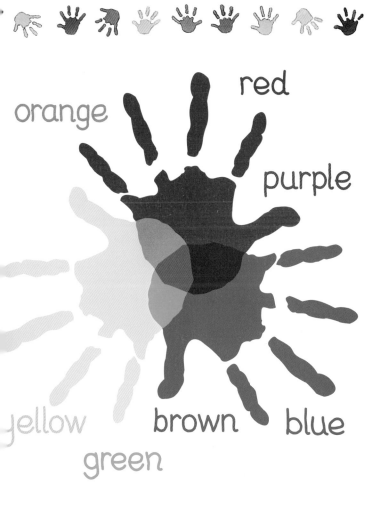

orange red purple yellow brown blue green

Red, blue and yellow make brown.

Help your child to create new colours by mixing paints.

Everything around us has a shape.
This train track is circle shaped.

It goes round and round.

Trace round each circle shape with your finger.

button

cake

wheel

ball

These tiles are triangle shaped.
They each have three corners.

Can you point to all three corners?

How many triangles can you
see here?

cheese

sails

pizza

party hat

These blocks are square shaped.

What colour squares can you see?

Let's go on a square hunt!

painting

window

puzzle

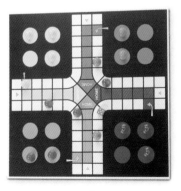

game board

This tile is rectangle shaped.

Can you see how it is different from a square?

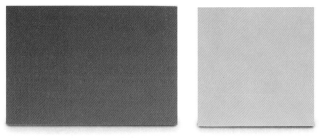

rectangle   square

Talk to your child about the differences between a rectangle (two sides long and two sides short) and a square (all sides are the same length).

Can you find these rectangles in your house?

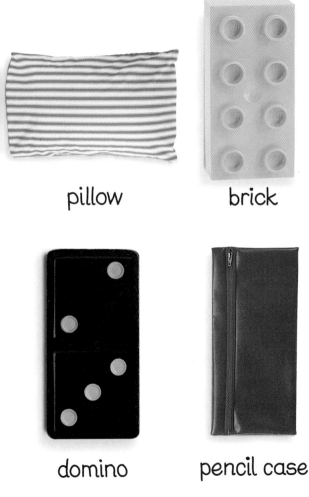

pillow

brick

domino

pencil case

A feast of colours and shapes, what a treat! Say the names of the shapes you'd like to eat.

First Steps

Aimed at children aged 2 years and upwards, the **First Steps** range of mini hardback books, activity books and flash cards are designed to complement one another and can be used in any order.

mini hardbacks

- abc
- 123
- colours and shapes
- sorting and opposites
- time

  Durable hardback books use photographs and illustrations to introduce important early learning concepts.

from **First Steps** *abc*